Explore Space!

Satellites

by Kathleen W. Deady

Consultant:
James Gerard
Aerospace Education Specialist
NASA Aerospace Education Services Program

Bridgestone Books
an imprint of Capstone Press
Mankato, Minnesota

Bridgestone Books are published by Capstone Press
151 Good Counsel Drive, P.O. Box 669, Mankato, Minnesota 56002
http://www.capstone-press.com

Copyright © 2003 by Capstone Press. All rights reserved.
No part of this publication may be reproduced in whole or in part, or stored in a retrieval system, or transmitted in any form or by any means, electronic, mechanical, photocopying, recording, or otherwise, without written permission of the publisher.
For information regarding permission, write to Capstone Press,
151 Good Counsel Drive, P.O. Box 669, Dept. R, Mankato, Minnesota 56002
Printed in the United States of America.

Library of Congress Cataloging-in-Publication Data
Deady, Kathleen W.
    Satellites / by Kathleen W. Deady.
    p. cm.—(Explore space!)
    Summary: An introduction to the history and various uses of artificial satellites.
    Includes bibliographical references and index.
    ISBN 0-7368-1400-0 (hardcover)
    1. Artificial satellites—Juvenile literature. [1. Artificial satellites.] I. Title. II. Series.
TL796.3 .D43 2003
629.46—dc21   2001008682

Editorial Credits
Christopher Harbo, editor; Karen Risch, product planning editor; Steve Christensen, series designer; Patrick D. Dentinger, book designer; Kelly Garvin, photo researcher

Photo Credits
Corbis/Bettmann, 6
Digital Vision, cover (satellite image)
Lockheed Martin Missiles & Space, 10
NASA, 4, 8, 12, 14, 18, 20
NOAA, 16
PhotoDisc, Inc., cover (Earth image)

1 2 3 4 5 6 07 06 05 04 03 02

Table of Contents

Satellites 5
The First Artificial Satellite 7
Satellites Today 9
Launching a Satellite 11
Orbiting Earth 13
Communication Satellites 15
Weather Satellites 17
Military Satellites 19
Space Science Satellites 21
Hands On: Launching a Satellite 22
Words to Know 23
Read More 24
Internet Sites 24
Index 24

Satellites

Satellites are objects that travel around Earth, other planets, or the Sun. Satellites may be natural like the Moon. They also can be artificial. People build artificial satellites. Artificial satellites help people learn about Earth and space.

The First Artificial Satellite

Sputnik was the first artificial satellite. The former Soviet Union launched Sputnik in 1957. Sputnik was a metal ball the size of a large beach ball. It weighed 184 pounds (83 kilograms). Sputnik sent radio signals to Earth.

signal
a sound or picture sent to or from a satellite

Students from around the world helped polish the 845 mirrors on STARSHINE 2.

STARSHINE 2

Satellites Today

More than 2,500 satellites orbit Earth today. Satellites send TV and radio signals around the world. Scientists use satellites to study the weather. They also use satellites to study outer space. Governments use satellites to watch other countries.

orbit
to travel around a planet or the Sun

Launching a Satellite

Three-stage rockets often carry satellites into space. The first stage of the rocket lifts the satellite high in the air. The second stage takes the satellite even higher and faster. A third stage places the satellite into orbit. Astronauts also launch satellites from the space shuttle.

stage
a rocket engine that lifts objects into orbit

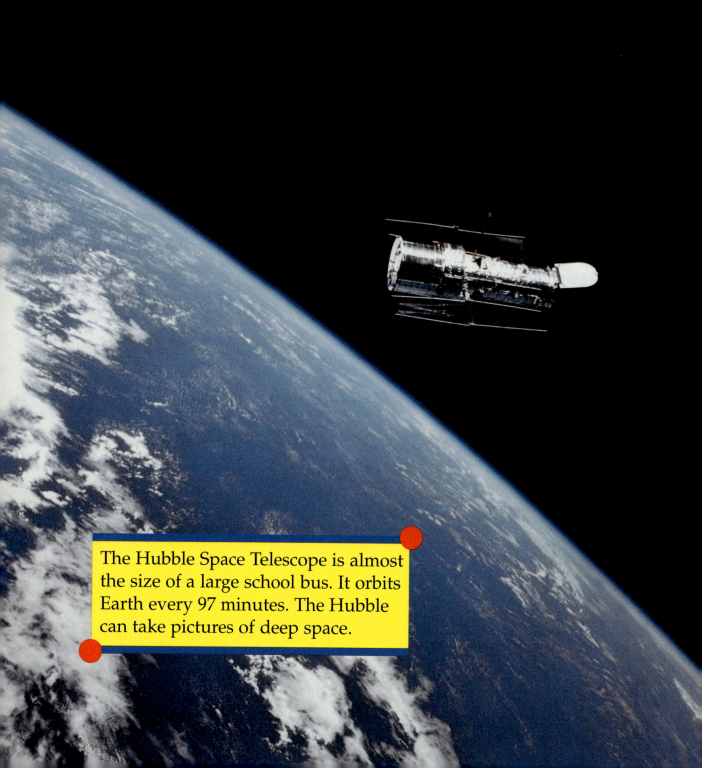

The Hubble Space Telescope is almost the size of a large school bus. It orbits Earth every 97 minutes. The Hubble can take pictures of deep space.

Orbiting Earth

Satellites orbit at different distances above Earth. Satellites 200 miles (320 kilometers) high can orbit Earth in 90 minutes. Satellites 22,300 miles (35,890 kilometers) high will orbit Earth in one day.

Communication Satellites

Communication satellites send TV, radio, and telephone signals around the world. These satellites pick up the signals from Earth. They then send the signals back to receiving stations. Receiving stations use dish-shaped antennas to collect the signals.

antenna
a wire or dish that sends or receives signals

Weather satellites can see hurricanes as they form. Meteorologists combine satellite pictures with maps. They then can track the direction the storms travel.

Weather Satellites

Weather satellites carry cameras and other tools. The satellites track storms and take pictures of clouds on Earth. These satellites help meteorologists warn people about storms such as hurricanes and blizzards.

meteorologist
a person who studies the weather

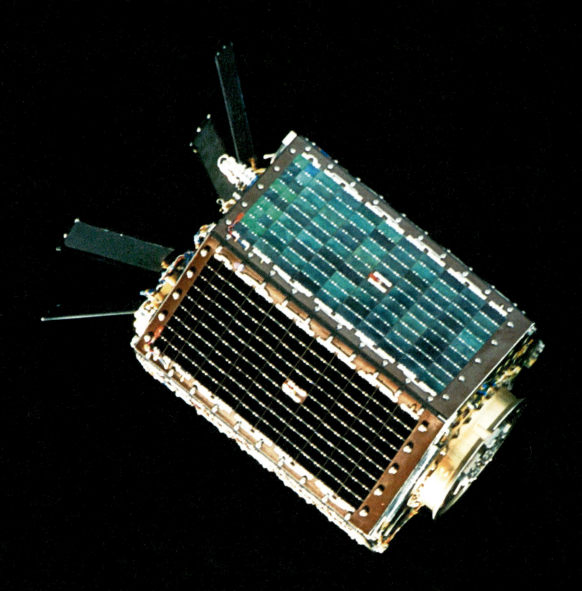

Military Satellites

Military satellites watch other countries. These satellites take pictures of military weapons such as guns and army trucks. The satellites send the pictures back to Earth. Military satellites warn countries when an army is about to attack.

military
part of the armed forces of a country

International Space Station

Space Science Satellites

Satellites help scientists learn about Earth and space. The Hubble Space Telescope takes pictures of other planets. It studies light from stars. The International Space Station is a very large satellite. Astronauts live in the space station and do experiments.

experiment
a test to learn something new

Hands On: Launching a Satellite

Rockets need to go very fast to put a satellite into orbit. Try this activity to find out why.

What You Need

Small ball   Masking tape
Table   Ruler

What You Do

1. Roll the ball very slowly off the table. Mark where the ball first bounces with the masking tape.
2. Roll the ball off the table again. Roll it a little faster this time. Again, mark where the ball first bounces.
3. Roll the ball a few more times. Roll the ball a little harder each time. Mark each landing with tape.
4. Use the ruler to measure between each mark on the floor. Does the ball go farther each time? How much farther does the ball go before it lands? Why?

A rocket must go very fast to put a satellite into space. It must travel fast enough to escape the force of gravity. Gravity is a force that pulls objects toward Earth. The same is true for the ball. The ball goes faster when you push it harder. It travels farther before gravity pulls it down. Imagine if you could throw the ball 17,000 miles (27,400 kilometers) per hour. That is how fast a rocket launches a satellite.

Words to Know

artificial (ar-ti-FISH-uhl)—made by people

astronaut (ASS-truh-nawt)—someone trained to fly into space in a spacecraft

launch (LAWNCH)—to send a spacecraft into space

satellite (SAT-uh-lite)—an object that circles Earth; many satellites are machines that take pictures or send telephone calls and TV programs to Earth.

signal (SIG-nuhl)—a sound or picture sent to or from a satellite

space shuttle (SPAYSS SHUT-uhl)—a spacecraft that carries astronauts into space and back to Earth

weapon (WEP-un)—anything used when fighting; guns, tanks, and bombs are weapons.

Read More

Mellett, Peter. *Launching a Satellite.* Expert Guide. Des Plaines, Ill.: Heinemann Library, 1999.

Stille, Darlene R. *Satellites.* Let's See. Minneapolis: Compass Point Books, 2002.

Internet Sites

Canadian Space Agency—Kid Space
http://www.space.gc.ca/kidspace/default.asp

NASA—Satellites
http://liftoff.msfc.nasa.gov/academy/rocket_sci/satellites

Index

antennas, 15
astronauts, 11, 21
communication, 15
experiments, 21
Hubble Space Telescope, 12, 21
International Space Station, 21
launch, 7, 11
meteorologists, 16, 17
military, 19
Moon, 5

orbit, 9, 11, 12, 13
receiving stations, 15
rocket, 11
scientists, 9, 21
signals, 7, 9, 15
space shuttle, 11
Sputnik, 7
storms, 16, 17
Sun, 5
weather, 9, 16, 17